Your Home Is a Learning Place

Pamela Weinberg

SIGNAL HILL

ATTENTION READERS: We would like to hear what you think about our books. Please send your comments or suggestions to:

Signal Hill Publications
P.O. Box 131
Syracuse, NY 13210-0131

SIGNAL HILL

© 1993 Signal Hill Publications
A publishing imprint of Laubach Literacy International

Content reviewer: Kevin Noel, M.S.

9 8 7 6 5 4 3 2

Library of Congress Cataloging-in-Publication Data

Weinberg, Pamela.
Your home is a learning place / Pamela Weinberg.
ISBN 0-88336-641-X
1. Education, Preschool—Parent participation. 2. Education,
Preschool—Activity programs. 3. Reading (Preschool)—
Parent participation. I. Title.
[LB1139.35.P37W45   1993]
649' .68—dc20   93-423
                                          CIP

Contents

Acknowledgments

This book is dedicated to my parents, Susan Baer and the late Walter N. Baer; my husband, Alan Weinberg; and to my children, Nathan and David Weinberg, who have helped me to grow and learn.

With heartfelt thanks and appreciation to these people who shaped this book with their ideas and dedication to children and families:

Sue Chamberlin; Myrna Rubenstein; Barye Deel; Lillie B. Stein; Esther Ann Zabitz; Milton Zabitz; Ann Marie Lapkowicz; Sheila Carson; Cindy Shiraki, OTR/L; Wilma Soliday, CCC-SLP; Margaret Malehorn; Patty Armbrust; and Judith Mansbarger.

To the Reader

You are your child's first and most important teacher. Your child learns all kinds of things from you. What he learns at home can make a big difference when he starts school. If your child is already in school, you can still help him learn. You do not need a high school or college degree to be a good teacher for your child. What you do need is time and caring.

This book suggests ways to help your child learn at home. You may already be doing some of these things. As this book will show, daily life offers many chances to teach your child. You can use common household items as learning tools. You do not have to sit with workbooks. You do not have to spend a lot of money.

This book is not about how to help your child with schoolwork. The teaching ideas given here are supposed to help you teach your child some basic skills. A child with good basic skills will be prepared to do well in school.

Of course, helping with homework is important. Before you help your child, make sure he tries the work alone. Then you can work together. You can set a daily time for homework. Make sure there is a good place for you both to work. If you have trouble giving help, ask a friend. Or ask the teacher what you can do.

Reading and writing are some of the basic skills this book covers. You will find ways to practice listening, speaking, and math skills. You can learn how your child can become a careful observer and build his memory. And you can find ways for your child to express himself through drama and art.

Parents are not the only ones who will be able to use this book. Anyone who cares for young children might find it helpful. This could mean grandparents, aunts, uncles, or baby-sitters.

Ideas in the chapters that follow are mainly for children about 5 to 11 years old. Not everyone in this age group will be able to do each activity. Some activities are harder than others.

You may find the letter **A**, **B**, or **C** printed after an activity. The easiest activities are marked with an **A**. The hardest ones are marked with a **C**. Use these letters as a guide. Just remember that you are the best judge of what your child can do.

Give some of the ideas in this book a try. Your home is a learning place. Making the most of it can be rewarding and fun.

Observe and Remember

Some people are good observers. They watch the world around them closely. They notice a lot of details.

People with good memories remember many facts and names. They remember a lot about what they see and hear.

Being able to observe and remember well are thinking skills. They are important skills for kids to use often.

A child who is a good observer is able to focus her mind. This can help her do work without making a lot of mistakes. It can help her solve problems and pay attention in school.

A strong memory helps kids, too. Memory skills are also needed in school. Test grades often depend on how well a child remembers facts.

Help your child practice observing and remembering. These skills get better with use.

Observation

Match Socks

Make a game of sorting clean clothes. Your child can help you match socks. This teaches how to tell things that are alike. Ask your child to tell you how the socks are alike and different. **A**

Match Cards

This game teaches kids to concentrate. It is a matching game played with a deck of cards. Players must use their memories to match cards.

Put all of the cards face down, one by one. Take turns picking two cards to turn over. Match cards that have the same number or face value. Every time you match a pair, put them in a pile. Each person's turn lasts until a match is not made. Play until all the cards are gone. The person with the most pairs at the end wins. **B**

"Guess What I See"

This is a good game to play outdoors as well as indoors. Play it while waiting in line or walking. Begin by picking an object and saying, "Guess what I see." Your child should then ask questions to find out what the object is.

Child: *"What color is it?"*

Parent: *"Red."*

In this example, the parent is talking about a stop sign.

This teaches children to ask questions and come up with answers. Let your child make as many guesses as he needs to get the right answer. Then it is his turn to say, "Guess what I see." **A B C**

Textures around Us

Your child may enjoy finding different textures. Ask her to find something soft (a flannel shirt), smooth (window glass), or rough (a brick in the wall). Ask her to find something scratchy (a heavy wool sweater) or bumpy (the bottom of a shoe). Discuss how the textures are different. **A**

Colors

Have your child name the colors of objects you point out. Give help if needed. **A**

Memory

Hidden Object

This game lets children use their sense of touch. Get a large bowl or pot. Fill it two inches or more with dried beans, rice, packing material, cornmeal, dry pasta shapes, or oatmeal.

Put an object in the bowl or pot. Bury the object so it cannot be seen. Have your child reach into the container and try to find what you hid. Ask him to guess what the object is as soon as he feels it. Things to hide might be a spoon, toy car, hair barrette, wrapped piece of candy, key, or coin.

This game should not be played with very young children. They could put small objects in their mouths and choke. Any child who plays this game should be watched closely. **A B**

Rhythms to Remember

Find a tall glass or jar, and a pencil. On the glass or jar, tap out a rhythm with the pencil. Have your child take the pencil and tap the same pattern. Next, your child can make up a new rhythm for you to repeat. You might try to tap out part of a song you know.

This activity helps kids learn to remember what they hear. Also, learning to hear sound patterns can improve the way a person forms sentences. **A B**

Words from A to Z

Two or more people can play this game. The first player says a word that starts with the letter A (for example, *apple*). The second player repeats the word for A. Then she adds a word for B (*apple, bell*). On every turn, a player repeats all the words said before and adds a word for the next letter in the alphabet (*apple, bell, car, . . .*). This improves memory skills. It also helps kids learn words. **C**

Sequences

A sequence is a series of things that are in a certain order. Ask your child to listen as you say a sequence of items. Then have him repeat what you said. This builds listening and memory skills.

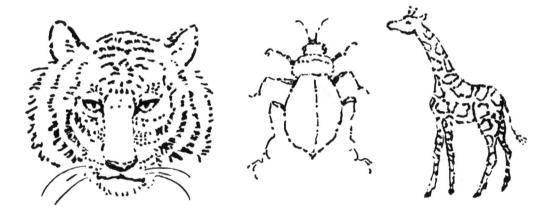

Start with a small number of items. For example, say two or three letters (*a-b-c*), numbers (*1-2-3*), or words (*tiger, beetle, giraffe*). As your child's skills improve, try a sequence of five to seven items. Also try having him repeat the sequence backwards. **B C**

Read and Remember

Pick an ad or short article that interests your child. Read it yourself, then have your child read it out loud or silently. Once she is finished, take it away. Ask some simple questions about the ad or article. This can show how well your child remembers and understands what she reads. **C**

A Minute to Remember

This activity is good for children of all ages. Select a picture from a magazine or newspaper. Let your child look at it for one minute. Have him say what he sees. (It will help his memory.) Then take the picture away. Find out how many things in the picture he can remember. This tests how well he remembers what he sees. **B C**

Memorize

Help your child memorize a joke, a poem, or a saying. You can share with her something you already know by heart. Or you can read something to her. Start with an item that is short or simple. One or two sentences is fine. Nursery rhymes work well. Her phone number and address are good to try, too. Children can work their way up to longer items later. **A B C**

Reading

In childhood and beyond, reading opens doors. The earlier a child is around reading, the better.

Kids need to read in school. They have to read textbooks and papers. They have to read directions and questions on tests. To do well in almost any subject, a child must use reading skills.

Reading outside of school is important, too. Kids need to read all kinds of things, from notes and signs to movie listings.

By reading, kids learn new words. They learn new ways to express ideas and feelings.

Reading also gives kids a way to explore the world. A child may not be able to visit China. But he can read a book about it. He can visit China in his mind.

Make reading a part of your child's life at home. Like playing, treat reading as a fun thing to do. Make it a family activity. Before long, your child will love it.

Learning about Letters

The ABCs

One part of learning to read is getting to know the letters in the alphabet. Help your child learn the names of the letters. Say the whole alphabet with her. Sing the alphabet song if you know it.

Soon your child will be able to say the ABCs back to you. Once she can point to letters when named, tell her some of the sounds the letters make. Work with just one or two letters at a time so she does not get confused.

Repeat and build upon what your child has learned. With your child, find letters on things you see every day. Look on cereal boxes and signs.

Once a child knows the ABCs, learning to spell her own name is a fun way to work with letters. Be creative in teaching your child how to spell her name. Kids often like to play with magnetic letters or with letters made out of felt, fabric, or paper. **A**

Magic Letter Box

Make a "magic letter box." You probably have in your home all the things you will need. Find a tray or box with low sides, like the top of a shoebox. You might want to glue a piece of dark paper inside on the bottom.

Pour two to three tablespoons of flour, sugar, or sand in the box. Your child can practice tracing and making letters with his finger. **A**

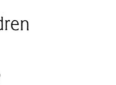

Books

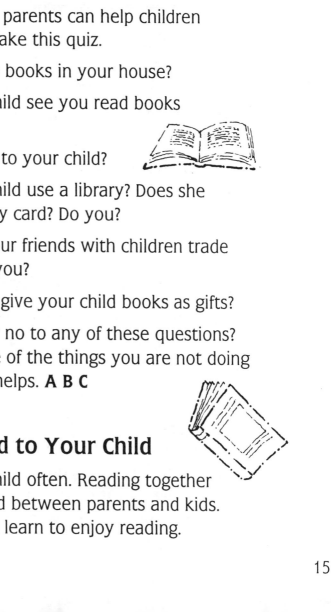

Building Interest in Books

There are ways parents can help children become readers. Take this quiz.

- Do you keep books in your house?
- Does your child see you read books or papers?
- Do you read to your child?
- Does your child use a library? Does she have a library card? Do you?
- Do any of your friends with children trade books with you?
- Do you ever give your child books as gifts?

Did you answer no to any of these questions? If so, try doing one of the things you are not doing now. Every effort helps. **A B C**

Read to Your Child

Read to your child often. Reading together builds a close bond between parents and kids. Kids feel good and learn to enjoy reading.

Before you read a page in a book, ask your child to look at the pictures. Ask him to tell you what is happening. Let your child "read" the pictures to you.

Use your finger sometimes to point to words as you read them aloud. Move your finger below the words. This helps your child learn to connect the word he hears with one he sees in print.

When your child has heard a story enough times, let him "read" it to you. For young children, telling the story is what matters. They do not have to get every word right.

Teach children to take care of books. It is important for kids to be careful with library books. If a book belongs to your child, let him write his name in it. This may help him feel that books have value.

Make books seem special. Give one to your child as a gift. Write something to him inside the front cover. **A B**

Reading on Their Own

Many older children are able to read on their own. As a parent, you can still be involved with an older child's reading.

Ask questions about what your child reads. Help her figure out what some words mean. Get a dictionary if you can. A small paperback dictionary is fine. Help your child look up words. Let her know that it is OK if a person does not know something. It is good to ask questions and look for answers.

Talk about a special interest or hobby your child has. Then try to find books or magazines about it. What a child reads is not what matters most. What does matter most is simply that she is reading.

If you read something interesting, you may want to share it with your child. Sometimes you and your older child can read to each other. **C**

Other Things to Read

Greeting Cards

Give your child cards on his birthday. Give cards at other special times. Greeting cards are fun to get. They show how words can be used to express feelings.

Kids can save cards to read again. Find a box to keep cards in. Your child can decorate the box.

Help your child pick cards to give to other people. Read cards together at the store.

Making your own greeting cards can be fun. First, your child should fold a piece of paper. Then he can write a message and draw pictures. He can cut pictures out of a magazine to glue on the paper. Or he can cut out words and use them to make sentences on the card. **A B C**

Charts and the TV Guide

Looking at the TV guide can help kids learn to read charts. Often, the names of programs are in small boxes on a chart. The times that programs start may be at the top. The stations you can watch may be listed on the chart's left side.

Ask what your child's favorite show is. Help her find the show on the chart. Ask her to tell you what time it starts. Ask what other shows are on at that time. **B C**

	8:00	8:30	9:00
2	Search for Clues, Mystery		Sports
4	Sandy's Place	Champion Car Races	
7	Kids and Kites	Firefighter's Story	Police Work
9	A Look at Monkeys	Ocean Adventures	

The Funny Pages

Read comic strips in the newspaper with your child. Collect favorite comics. Post them in places where they can be seen and enjoyed.

Cut a comic strip out of the newspaper. Then cut the strip apart. Each piece should be one frame, or box. Mix up the frames. Ask your child to put them back in order. **B**

Label Your House

Put labels on furniture and other household items. For example, write the word *chair* on a piece of paper and tape it to a chair. This helps children learn to spell the names of things. **B**

Writing

Writing is a way to put thoughts on paper. At home or in school, kids need to write.

Writing helps us remember things. We jot down dates we have to remember. We keep addresses and phone numbers. We make lists.

Writing also helps us share information and ideas with others. We send notes and letters. Some people write stories and poems.

Students have to be able to write for school. They have to give written reports. They have to do homework and take tests.

If a person does not do it a lot, writing can seem hard. Get your child to write as much as possible. Show how many different ways you can use writing.

Give your child the chance to express feelings on paper. She may find that writing can be more than just useful. It can be something to enjoy.

Get Ready to Write

Build Hand Muscles to Write

People need muscle control to write. Before your child learns to write, there are many ways to build his hand muscles.

Using tools develops hand muscles. Your child may enjoy trying out different tools. You may be surprised to find how many tools you already have at home. There is no need to buy new tools or toys to get your child ready to write.

Teach your child to use different kitchen tools. He can sift flour with a sifter, lift cookies from a tray with a spatula, or serve vegetables with a big spoon. He can beat eggs with an eggbeater, spread butter with a butter knife, or pour milk from a pitcher.

As a child uses tools, his hands grow stronger. Later, when he needs to hold a pencil to write, he will be ready. **A**

Drawing and Coloring

A child's first marks on paper are the beginnings of writing. As a child scribbles and draws, she learns the pleasure of putting something on paper.

Coloring gets a child used to a writing tool. As a child colors with crayons, she learns to control her hand movements. She learns to put marks at a certain place on a page.

If you want, get your child coloring books with pictures to color in. Or just give her crayons and paper and let her imagination take over. **A B**

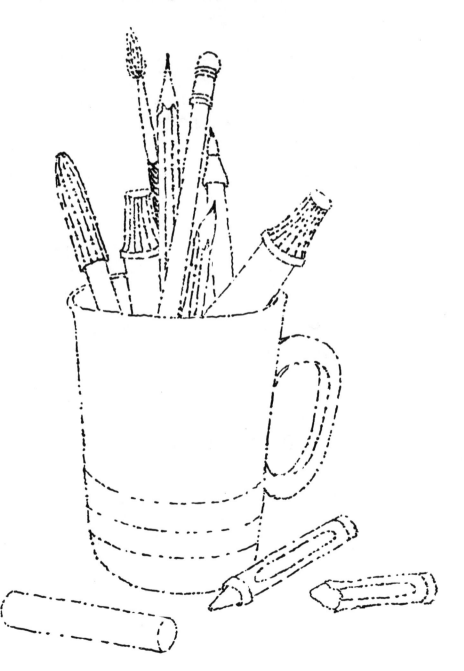

Putting Words on Paper

Your Child's Story in Print

Have your child tell you a story. Perhaps it can go along with pictures he has drawn. Write down the story as he tells it. You do not have to write every sentence exactly as he says it. Just get the sense of the story. Later, read it back to him.

Writing down what your child says is called *taking dictation*. It shows your child first-hand that talk can be written down and then read.

Children enjoy hearing, seeing, and reading their own words. It shows them that their thoughts and feelings are important to people around them. **A B**

Show Support for Writing

Let your child see you write. Make a grocery list, mark a date on a calendar, or copy a name and phone number. Kids who see parents write learn that writing is important.

Keep writing supplies in the house. This makes children more likely to write. A child will feel that you support her efforts. Pencils, a pencil sharpener, pens, crayons, markers, and different kinds of paper are some supplies you could keep. **A B C**

Your Bathroom Is a Writing Place

People sing in the bathroom. Why not write in the bathroom? Look around when the room is steamy. Find fog on the mirror or mist on the side of the tub. A young child can make letters or pictures there with his finger. An older child can write messages. **A B**

Mail

Relatives and friends who cannot visit much will like getting mail. You and your child can address an envelope or postcard. Take a trip to the post office or a store to buy stamps. Then show your child where to find a mailbox.

```
Your Full Name
Street Address
City, State, ZIPcode

                Mr. Robert Dixon
                1414 Elm Dr.
                Brooktown, GA 12435
```

Here is how to address the outside of an envelope. Your name and address go in the upper left corner. This is called the return address. It tells the post office where to return the letter if there is a problem. The name and address of the person you are sending the letter to goes in the center of the envelope.

Help your child get an address book. Then she has somewhere to keep addresses of her friends and relatives. If you do not want to buy an address book, you can make one.

Staple together sheets of paper so there is a page for each letter of the alphabet. Write letters on the top of each page. This shows where to put addresses of people whose last names begin with each letter.

Children can draw pictures or cartoons to send with their letters. Or they can send artwork only. Children who are too young to write can draw.

Your child may enjoy sending pictures from a magazine. She can paste the pictures on paper and write comments or captions. Recipes and articles also can be shared. **A B C**

Writing in School

Children often bring home papers they worked on in school. These papers are important to save. Your child has put a lot of effort into them.

Sometimes papers show that children took time to do neat and accurate work. Sometimes children try hard but do not get good grades.

Keep your child's papers, both good and bad. This will let him know that it is all right to make mistakes. He will feel that his efforts are worthy. This also shows that the written word has value. The papers can be a record of your child's progress, too.

A simple file folder is a good place to keep school papers. Label the outside of the folder with your child's name, grade, and teacher's name.

Before putting the papers away, you can go over them with your child. Talk about errors and about what he did well. This shows that schoolwork is important and that you care about how your child is doing. **A B C**

Notes at Home

Have children write notes to other family members. A note can remind someone to do something. It can tell that a friend phoned while you were out.

Often you can just tell a person about a message. It still helps to write messages down, too. That way, people are less likely to forget what they need to know.

Sometimes it is nice to surprise a person with notes. The notes can have messages that let the reader know you care about her. Leave notes for your child in places she will not expect. Slip a note into a sandwich bag. Put a note inside a shoe. Keep the messages simple. "You're a great kid" could be enough for one note. **B C**

Make a Book

Kids can make their own books. Staple blank pieces of paper together. Your child can then draw a picture on each page. He can write a story to go along with the pictures. Help him write the story if needed. A homemade book could be a fun gift for your child to give someone. **B C**

Journals

A journal is a written record of what a person does and thinks. A journal can also be called a diary. Keeping one is a good way to practice writing. Journals give people a chance to reflect on life. And they can be fun to read years later.

Many older children enjoy journals. Find out if your child would like to keep one. Tell her that a journal is private. People should share their writing with others only if they want to. Explain that a journal is a place where people can write anything they want. They do not have to worry about mistakes. Some people like to include poems or drawings in their journals.

Get a notebook for your child to write in. If you want, find a special book for her to use. You could give this as a gift. Bookstores often sell blank books. You may be able to find a diary with a lock. Check a store that sells writing supplies.

You can help a younger child keep a journal. Get a notebook and ask your child to tell you about her day. Write down what she says. Each day, add new stories. Be sure to date each entry. **B C**

Autograph Books

An autograph book is a book a child gets his friends to write in. Writing in an autograph book means more than just signing your name. You can write a funny poem. You can tell a friend what you find special about him. Kids often like the chance to write for each other.

A plain notebook is just fine to use for an autograph book. Or you can staple pieces of paper together to make one. Have your child decorate the cover. **B C**

Be a Critic

Start your own "critic's corner." Ask your child to write comments on what he likes or dislikes about a TV show or movie. This gives him a chance to express opinions in writing. **C**

Author, Author

After your child has watched a movie or TV show, ask her to write a different ending to the story. This is a creative way for her to use words. It gives her a chance to take an idea in a new direction. **C**

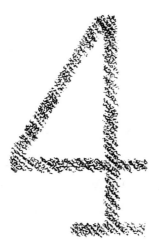

Listening and Speaking

Most of us are able to listen and speak. We may do so almost without thinking. Yet listening and speaking are skills we can practice.

We all know good speakers. How did they get that way? Most likely, they had lots of practice. They got many chances to learn and use words. You can give your child chances to learn and use words. This can help him become better at expressing himself through speech.

Listening is a skill people often take for granted. But not everyone is a good listener. Careful listening takes work. Like other skills, though, it gets easier with practice.

Being able to listen and speak well is good for kids. They will not miss things their teacher says in school. They can ask and answer questions clearly. They can enjoy talking with others. And when they speak, they will be able to feel sure of themselves.

Vocabulary Building

Naming

You can help your child become a better speaker by building her vocabulary. A person's speaking vocabulary is all the words she knows and can use when speaking.

As you do tasks around the house, teach your child the names for everyday things. This is one way to build a young child's speaking vocabulary.

Ask your child to name objects in a room. Or ask her to name things in a picture or along the street. As you make a meal, ask her to name ingredients. If she does not know a name, tell her what word to use. **A**

Rhyming Words

Play a rhyming game with your child. One person says a word to start the game. Then another person says a word that rhymes with the first word. Players take turns adding words that rhyme (for example, *cat-rat-bat-sat*). A word may be used only once. The winner is the last person who can think of a rhyming word. **B**

Listen and Tell

Question Game

For fun, ask your child to listen to some questions and then to answer with yes, no, or maybe. You can use the questions below, and then make up your own. This activity gets children to listen and think about what other people say. **A**

- Can you pick up an elephant?
- Can you pick up a suitcase?
- Does ice feel cold?
- Do you wear a hat on your feet?
- Are you a girl?

Exact Words

Have your child whisper a sentence or two in your ear. Then say a sentence or two back to him. You can repeat exactly what he said. Or you can make up something. Have your child tell if you said the same words he did.

Next, it is your turn to give the whispered message. This game gets kids to pay close attention to what they say and hear. **B**

When We Ask and Answer

Children often use questions and answers to talk with people outside the family. As a parent, you can help your child talk more clearly.

Sometimes a one-word answer to a question is fine. But often it is better to answer with more words. By giving longer answers, children build speaking skills. They get the chance to put more thought into what they say.

Here is a question that a child could answer with one word.

Parent: *Are you upstairs?*

Child: *Yes.*

Here is a question that a child could use more words to answer. This question makes a child give specific details.

Parent: *What are you doing upstairs?*

Child: *I'm looking for my baseball bat.*

Think about how you as a parent ask questions. Also think about how you answer questions. Be clear and simple when explaining something. Try to give your child the right amount of information. Too many details or too few can be confusing. **A B C**

On the Phone

Phone Talk

Children can use the phone to practice listening and speaking. A very young child can play with a toy phone. She can pretend to talk with someone. Let your child make real phone calls when she is able. Have her call a friend or relative. **A B**

Take a Message

Older children can answer the phone and take phone messages. Children should know what to say when a caller wants someone who is not home. They should listen closely so they understand the message. They should also try to write the message.

Child: *Hello?*

Caller: *Is Mr. Carlton there?*

Child: *He can't come to the phone now. May I take a message?*

Caller: *Yes. Tell him that Joe Sweet called. I need to talk to him before 10 o'clock tomorrow morning.*

Child: *OK. I'll let him know. Let me make sure I got the message right. Joe Sweet needs to talk with him before 10 o'clock tomorrow morning. Does he have your phone number?*

Caller: *I think so, but I'll leave it now so I can be sure. It's 554-1756.*

Child: *OK, that's 554-1756. I'll pass it along.*

Caller: *Thank you.*

Here is the message the child wrote.

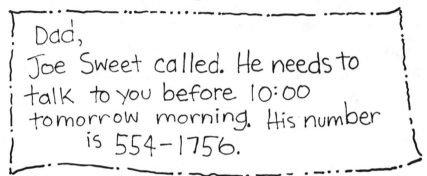

Dad,
Joe Sweet called. He needs to talk to you before 10:00 tomorrow morning. His number is 554-1756.

Notice that the child asked for the caller's name and phone number. When taking a message, a child should always get at least that information. **C**

Play It Again

On Tape

If you have a cassette player, your child can listen to cassette tapes. Many recordings are made just for kids. Try different ones and see what your child enjoys.

Look for books on tape in the library or bookstore. Try to find books with read-along tapes. A read-along tape is a recording of a person reading the book. These help children connect the words they hear with the words they read on a page. **A B C**

Tape It Yourself

Help your child make his own recordings. Get blank cassette tapes. Show how to use the tape player to record.

Your child can make many kinds of recordings. He can make a "letter on tape" for someone. He can record a story as he tells it. He can also make a tape of sound effects. One sound effect could be a door slamming. Another could be the shower running. Have your child play the finished tape for you. Guess what each sound is. **B C**

Music

Find recordings of music your child likes. Or listen to the radio with her. Sometimes children do not understand all the words to songs. Help your child understand them. Explain what the words are and what they mean.

Have fun with music. Dance. Clap to the beat. Sing along. Make up funny words to well-known songs. **A B C**

Talk, Talk, Talk

The Value of Talk

Talking with your child is important. Try to do it as much as you can. Just by talking with you, your child learns new words. The more kids speak, the better their speaking skills get.

Ask your child questions. Find out his thoughts and feelings. Listen closely to what he says. Then, respond to show you understood. Your child will know that you value what he thinks.

Comment on what happens in the world around you. Talk about what you see on TV. Talk about things you like. **A B C**

Actions and Words

Find chances to have your child explain things. She can tell you how to get someplace. The place could be a room in the house or a cabinet where dishes are kept.

Ask your child to explain each step in a task as she does it. You also can explain each step in jobs you do around the house. This models for your child how to put thoughts and actions into words. **A B C**

Walk through My Day

Your child might enjoy taking you for a "walk" through his day. Ask him to tell what happened in school. Find out what the class studied that day. This is a good way to help him remember what is going on in school.

Find out about places your child went. Find out about people he saw.

Tell him about your day. This will give your child a window into the world of adults. Talk about something you enjoyed. Be honest if something bad happened. Talk about ways to try to solve problems. Try to stress the good side of your day. **A B C**

Telling Family Stories

Tell your child stories about your life or the lives of relatives and close friends. This teaches the art of storytelling. It also can make family ties stronger.

Ask your child to tell you stories about her life. She needs to use her memory to tell a story. She has to organize her thoughts. She also gets to practice using words she knows.

Your child can tell you about things she has done. She can talk about a trip she took. She might describe something funny she saw. **A B C**

The Future Me

Have your child make up a story to tell you. It should describe his life as it could be years in the future. Ask questions for your child to answer in the role of his grown-up self. **C**

Build a Story

Build a story, sentence by sentence. This can be done by two people or a group. One person says a sentence to start the story. Then each person adds a sentence. Record the story on tape or write it down so that it can be saved. **A B C**

Math

Every day, your child sees math in action. At home or in school, children need to see how math is part of daily life. Numbers are used when answering many of the questions children ask.

- What time does my school bus pick me up?
- How long will it take to get there?
- How many more days until my birthday?
- Do I have enough money to buy the candy?

Math is much more than saying numbers in order from 1 to 100. It is more than adding and subtracting. Math is one way we make sense of what is happening in our lives.

Numbers

Get to Know Numbers

Numbers are all around us. Help your child get to know numbers. When you see a number somewhere, point it out. Discuss how it is being used. Read numbers on the clock, dates on the calendar, or room numbers in a school. Note how numbers are used for TV channels, radio stations, roads, and phone numbers. **A**

Count on Sports

Your child can learn numbers while playing sports. Toss a ball back and forth with your child. Count the number of tosses. Jump rope together, and count the number of jumps. **A B**

Sports give children of all ages the chance to practice math. Math is used in many ways in sports. We keep score with numbers. We clock speeds and measure distances. No matter what the game, math usually plays a part. **B C**

Count around the House

You and your child can find many things to count around the house. Count steps as you climb them or blocks as you stack them. Count buttons on a shirt, pages in a book, or cookies on a plate. Watch TV and count how many commercials are on during one show. Group items to count in different ways. For example, line up pairs of shoes and count by two's. Ask your child to think of other things to count. **A**

Weigh and Measure Yourself

Have your child keep track of her weight and height. Record the information on a chart each month. Add and subtract as needed to show changes. **B C**

Money, Money, Money

Real Money

Use real money to teach your child the names and values of different coins. Look in your wallet or pocket for loose change. Ask your child to help you sort the coins. Ask him to put all the same coins together and tell the name and value of each type. **A**

Show your child a coin. Ask him to find other coins that together are worth the same amount. For example: "Here is a dime. It is worth 10 cents. Show me other coins that add up to 10 cents." You also could say a certain amount of money and ask your child to show you that amount in real money. For example: "Show me 78 cents. Show me a dollar and 10 cents." **B**

Send an older child to the store with a list of items to buy. This teaches him to manage money. Give him $1, $5, $10, or some other appropriate amount. Ask to get change back. **C**

A Good Buy

Help your child plan to buy an item. Talk about making a budget. Figure out how much money is needed. How long will it take her to save the money? You may need to discuss how your child will get the money. Can you give her a little each week for doing tasks around the house? Can she earn money some other way?

If people want to save money for one thing, they may have to give up something else. Talk about what things your child might have to give up. **C**

If You Had the Money

Give your child a catalog to look at. It should have prices. A department store catalog would work well. Have your child pretend he has $150 to spend. Ask him to go through the catalog and decide what he could buy with the money. **C**

The Date and Time

Calendars

A calendar helps you keep track of appointments, holidays, birthdays, and other events. A calendar also can help teach math.

Put a calendar someplace at home where it is easy to see. Teach your child how to read it. In the morning, ask her to tell you the day's date. With your child, use the calendar to count the number of months in a year. Count the number of days in a month and a week. Figure out how many days there are until the next holiday. **A B**

Have your child figure out how many times per week or month she does certain things. How many times does she brush her teeth each week? How many days does she go to school each month? She can look at the calendar to figure out the answers. **C**

Give your child a calendar of her own. Some calendars are not expensive. Often, businesses give them away for free. Always keep a family calendar you write on yourself. That way, all family members can keep track of each other.

Tell the Time

Children can learn how to judge time. They can learn how to use the tools that measure time. A watch, alarm clock, wall clock, and kitchen timer are all tools that measure time. They help us know when to do what we need to do. Teach your child how to read and set clocks.

Ask your child to guess how long something will take. You might guess how long it will take to do the dishes or get to a friend's house. Note the starting time. Then note the ending time. How long did the activity take? How close was your child's guess? **A B**

Plan a Schedule

Help your child plan his daily schedule. Talk about what is supposed to happen and when.

For one day, help your child write down his schedule. First write the things he has to do. Write the times. Then let your child plan how to spend the rest of the time. **B C**

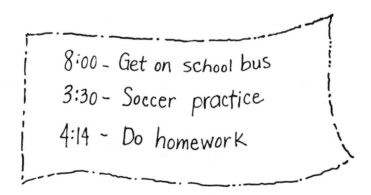

8:00 - Get on school bus
3:30 - Soccer practice
4:14 - Do homework

Time and the TV Guide

Use the TV guide to practice math skills. Have your child pick out a favorite show. What time does the show start? What time does it end? How long does it last? Pick out two other shows. Figure out how long each show lasts. Then add the lengths of the three shows. All together, how long do the shows last? **C**

Fractions in Action

Show your child how something can represent a fraction. Cut fruit or pie into equal sections. Explain that, when you cut a whole piece into two parts, each part is one half. Cut a whole piece into four parts to show quarters. Or cut a whole piece into three parts to show thirds.

You can also tear or cut a piece of paper into parts to show fractions. Or you can fold a napkin. Explain that using fractions can help us divide something equally among a group of people. **C**

Putting Skills Together

Often, you have to use more than one skill to get a job done. Picture a child taking a test in school. That child must read the test questions. He must write answers. Suppose part of the test confuses him. He must speak clearly as he asks the teacher questions. Then he must listen carefully to the teacher's answers.

Most of us are better at some things than other things. But there are times when we have to use both our stronger and weaker skills to do a job. Then we can see the value in practicing different kinds of skills.

Many common tasks give us a chance to use skills together. Some of these tasks are ones kids can take part in. Kids can help with cooking and shopping. They can spend time doing jigsaw puzzles and growing plants.

Cooking

Getting Ready to Cook

People use many skills when they cook. They read recipes and food labels. They follow directions and measure ingredients.

Kids can help a lot in the kitchen. Find a recipe to make with your child. Look in a cookbook, or ask a friend or relative for one. You will often find recipes with pictures and directions on the back of packages. Have your child help you decide what to make.

Use a recipe even if you already know how to prepare the dish. This will help your child learn.

Once you have chosen what to make, gather all of the things you need. Do not start cooking until you know you have everything.

Have your child get ingredients and cooking tools. Then read the ingredient list to her. She can double-check that all ingredients are there. Or she can be the reader and you can be the checker.

Read the whole recipe with your child before starting to cook. This helps you plan work and prevents mistakes.

Making the Dish

Help your child measure ingredients. Learning to measure builds math skills. Children can learn about fractions. They can learn different ways to measure things.

Let your child use kitchen tools as much as possible. Just keep safety in mind. A parent should do tasks where there may be danger. You, the parent, should do anything with sharp knives, stoves, ovens, or electric tools. Have your child work with spoons and other safe tools.

Following directions is an important part of cooking. Making a recipe is a lot like doing a science experiment. You must follow directions closely to get the right result. You must measure with care.

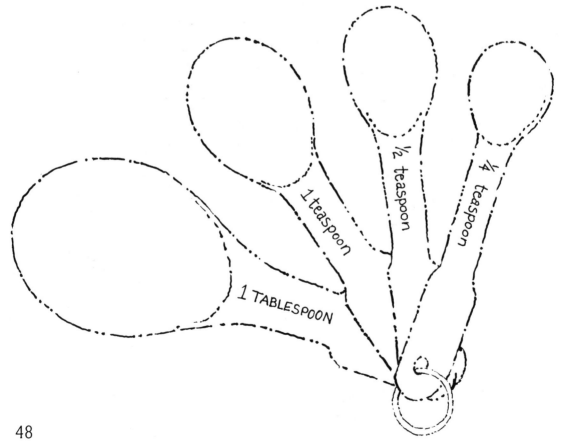

Cooking without a Recipe

Of course, you can make some dishes without following a recipe. This gives you and your child a chance to be creative cooks.

A salad is something that can be made without a recipe. You and your child can decide what to put in it. Try to pick vegetables of different colors, textures, and sizes. If you want, add eggs, cheese, or meat. Let your child help to clean and cut as much as he is able. Then have him put the ingredients into a bowl in layers.

Suppose the dish turns out to be very good. You may want to make it again sometime. Help your child write down a list of the ingredients used. You will have created your own recipe!

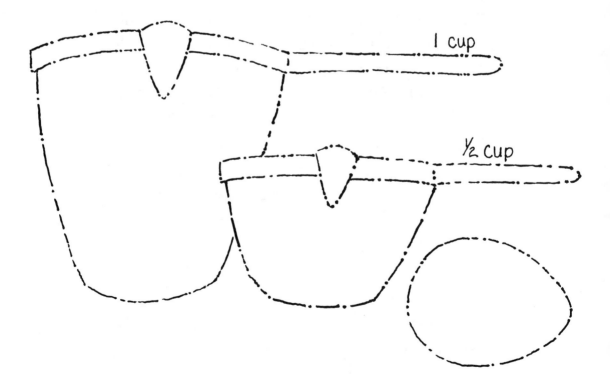

1 cup

½ cup

Puzzles

Doing Jigsaw Puzzles

Why play with jigsaw puzzles? There are many skills your child can learn. Doing jigsaw puzzles teaches children:

- to plan ahead
- to be organized
- to solve a problem
- to finish what you start
- to notice details

Many people enjoy jigsaw puzzles. One reason is because there are no hard directions to follow.

People with young children might not like jigsaw puzzles. This is because puzzle pieces can get scattered and lost. You should help your child keep puzzle pieces together. Teach her to take pieces out one at a time. If she dumps them out, they could scatter. She should set the pieces on a flat surface.

Tell your child first to try to guess where each piece goes. She should group pieces that seem to belong together. She could group them by colors or look for parts that connect. Then she can start putting the pieces together.

Try to help if your child has trouble finding puzzle pieces. Do puzzles along with your child at least a few times. This will build her confidence as she learns a new skill.

Set aside a little time during each week or month for doing puzzles. When your child finishes a puzzle, record the success in a puzzle "log." Tell how hard the puzzle was by how many pieces it had. You could write the date she did it and how long it took her. As time goes by, the log will show how much better she gets at doing puzzles.

Ask your child to be careful to put each piece away when she finishes with a puzzle. This teaches her to take care of her things. Also, pieces will not be missing when the time comes to put the puzzle together again.

Make Your Own Puzzles

You can buy puzzles in a store. Or you can help your child make his own. Cereal boxes are sturdy and colorful. Your child can glue a magazine picture onto the side of a cereal box. Or he can draw a picture to glue onto the box. After the glue is dry, cut the picture into pieces. A homemade puzzle could be a special gift for your child to give someone.

Sometimes, school supply stores or hobby stores sell blank puzzles. Your child can draw a picture or write a message on the puzzle.

Store puzzle pieces in a tray or bag. Keep puzzles organized by using a code to mark all of the pieces that belong together. For example, put a blue dot on the back of all the pieces that make up one puzzle.

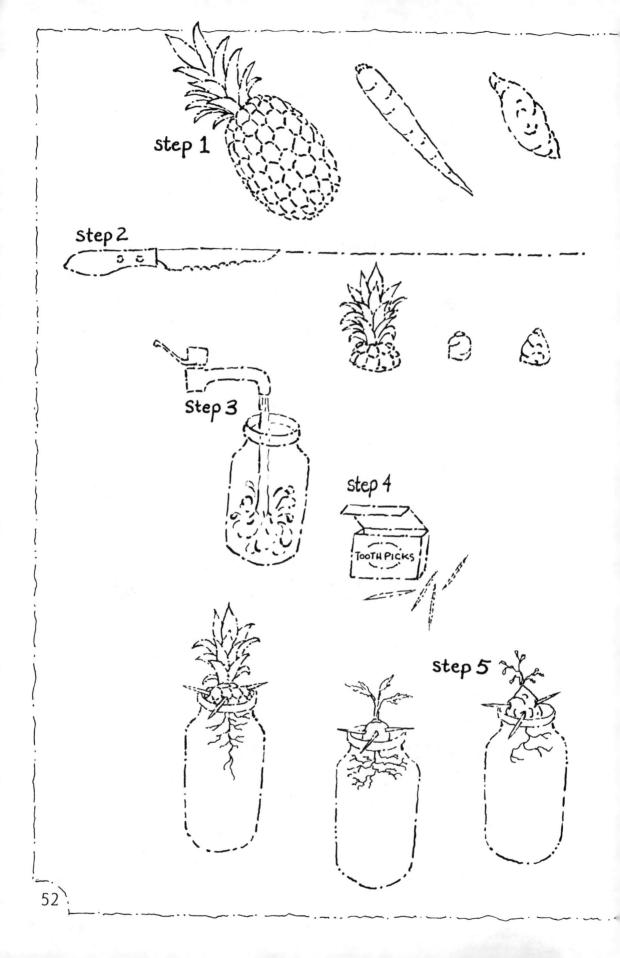

step 1

step 2

Step 3

step 4

TOOTH PICKS

step 5

52

Growing Plants

Growing plants at home gives kids a way of seeing the end result of something they start. You can plant seeds or bulbs. You can plant a cutting. You also can root vegetables or fruits. Then keep track of how the plant grows.

The fastest way to start a plant is from a rooted cutting. Soak the plants in water as shown. In a few weeks, roots will grow. Then put the plants in potting soil. Cover up the roots. Put the plant in a sunny place, and water it when it gets dry.

Your child can keep a growth chart for the plant. Each week, she can measure how much the plant has grown. She may wish to draw pictures to show how the plant changes. She also could write a story explaining how she grew the plant.

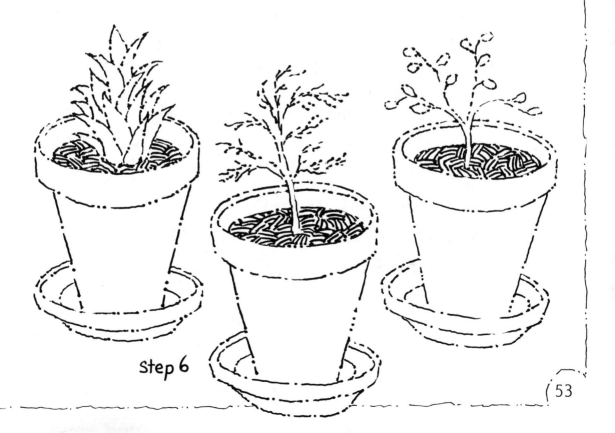

step 6

Shopping

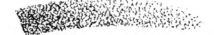

Make a Shopping List

Make a shopping list with your child. This shows how writing and reading can help you remember something later. An older child may be able to write the list with your help.

Before shopping, have your child try to memorize the list. When you get to the store, he tells what items to find. Keep the written list to make sure you do not forget an item. Make your child feel good about how many things he remembers. Do not let him feel bad if he forgets something. This is meant to be a game.

Sort Coupons

Coupons can help save money. They also can give your child a chance to practice sorting. With your child, look for coupons in newspapers or magazines. Then choose groups to use for sorting the coupons.

Some groups could be:

■ canned foods

■ dairy products

■ health and beauty aids

■ meats

Think of other groups to use. Sorting coupons can be hard. Some items seem to fit into more than one group.

You may want to put coupons into plain white envelopes. Write the name of one group on each of the envelopes.

Look over some coupons with your child. Ask the following questions. What product is a coupon for? How much money can you save? Is it for a product you buy often? How long is it good?

Reading in the Store

Read signs in the store. Point out and read the signs that tell what is in each part of the store. Read package labels. Ask your child to read a shopping list and help you find items on the shelves. If you have a coupon, ask your child to match it with a product.

Talking about Prices

Find where prices are marked. Some stores put price stickers right on items they sell. Other stores list prices on labels on the shelf. When you pick an item, read the price with your child. Older children can read prices to you.

Ask your child to notice different ways foods are measured to be sold. Some foods are measured by weight, with amounts shown in ounces or pounds. Liquids are measured by volume, with amounts shown in pints, quarts, or gallons. Some foods are measured by quantity.

They may be priced by the dozen, half-dozen, or number you get for a dollar. Help your child figure out what a certain amount of a product costs.

Your child can help weigh fruits and vegetables in the store. Weigh different sizes of a type of fruit or vegetable. Ask your child to tell which one weighs most. Ask her how much the fruit or vegetable costs per pound. Then see if she can tell how much a certain one will cost.

Discuss prices with your child. Ask her which of two items costs more. Compare prices of different brands of a food. Talk about the best buys. Are you willing to pay more to get a certain brand? What makes you choose one brand instead of another?

The Bill

As you shop, keep track of what the bill will be. Add prices together.

You may want to round off prices to the nearest 10 cents to make adding easier. For example, $1.08 rounded off to the nearest 10 cents would be $1.10. Rounding $1.35 to the nearest 10 cents would be $1.40.

People often round off numbers to make adding easier. Teach this idea to your child. Ask him to try rounding off some prices.

At the checkout counter, let your child pay for one or two small items separately. Have him figure out the cost. Then give him enough money to pay the bill. Have him tell you how much the change should be.

When you get the cash register receipt, look over it with your child. Look for the date. Locate item prices, tax, and the bill total. See if it shows how much money you gave and how much change you received.

Drama and Art

Kids need to show feelings. They need to be creative. Drama and art offer ways for kids to express themselves.

Through drama, kids get a chance to pretend to be someone else. They can play a role and see the world from a new point of view.

Through artwork, kids can express themselves without using words. They can draw pictures and make things of their own design.

Being creative is important in life. It helps people find new ways of doing things. It allows people to see problems from fresh angles.

Try to find ways to inspire your child's imagination. This chapter has a few ideas to get you started. There are many other things you can do. Look for ways to make artwork with items you have around the house. Have fun!

Drama

Act Out a Story

Children like to act out skits or make up plays. A box or basket can hold "costumes." Put in hats, aprons, jewelry, sports equipment, uniforms, scarves, or shirts.

Ask your child to act out scenes that are sad, funny, or scary. Have him assign parts to family members and friends. **A B C**

Charades for Children

To play charades (pronounced shuh-RAIDS), a person acts out something written on a slip of paper. This is the version for children to play. Write the names of things or people onto slips of paper. Write one name per slip. Mix up the slips. Then have your child pick one and act out what it says. You try to guess what person or thing the child picked. **B**

Statue

Play "statue." One person says the name of an activity. Another person freezes in the position of someone doing that activity. For example, one activity could be bowling. A person would pretend to be a statue of a bowler. **A B**

Puppets

Try making puppets. This can be as simple
as cutting out pictures and gluing them to sticks.
Then put on a puppet show. **A B C**

Art

Drawing

For younger children, scribbling is fun. They enjoy moving a crayon across paper. They like using their hands.

You can often find children making marks in dirt with a stick. You may even find them making marks on walls. It is a good idea to set up a place where children can draw on paper. It is also a good idea to keep crayons in a safe place.

Your child probably will like to draw with different colors. Try to keep crayons and markers in many colors.

At first, do not ask your child to draw a certain kind of picture. She might want to draw just lines and shapes. When she is ready to do more, she will show you. Let her move at her own pace. **A B**

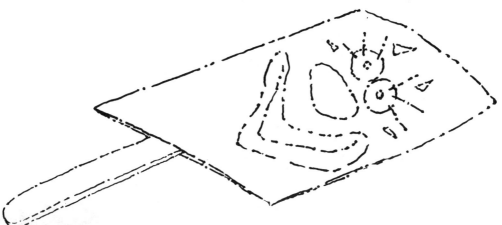

Surface Designs

Place a piece of paper over a textured surface. Rub a crayon over the paper. Rub gently or firmly. Try to use even pressure. Keep rubbing the crayon across the paper until you see a design. You can move the paper to make the design more interesting and unusual. **B C**

Surfaces to try:

Outdoors

- rocks

- bark on a tree

- sidewalk

- lettering on a sign

- cemetery marker

Indoors

- floors

- refrigerator

- window screen

- patterns in furniture

- cut-out figures in cardboard or stiff paper

Pasta Beads

String different pasta shapes on a pipe cleaner or piece of yarn. Make a necklace or bracelet. **A B**

A Place for Memories

Collect special photos. With your child, put them in a photo album. Write a caption under each one.

You may want to keep more than just photos. You can save letters, newspaper clippings, ticket stubs, or other special things. Paste everything into a scrapbook. Or you can put everything into a box. A "memory box" is good to use when not all objects are flat. **A B C**

A Flag of Your Own

Think of pictures and symbols that describe yourself. Use them to draw your own flag. **B C**

Final Thoughts

This book has offered some ideas for teaching your child at home. Do not stop with these. As you do special things with your child, you will come up with great ideas of your own. Think of how many ways your home can be a learning place. Share tips with other parents.

Some of your child's skills may be stronger than others. Try to do activities that will build weak skills.

Teaching your child at home can have wonderful results. When you spend time with your child, you show you care. Learning will be fun, not work. And a love of learning is something that can last throughout your child's life.